ETHEREUM

The Beginners Guide To Understanding Ethereum

Matthew Adams

Copyright © 2018 Matthew Adams

All rights reserved.

It is not legal to reproduce, duplicate, or transmit any part of this document in either electronic means or in printed format. Recording of this publication is strictly prohibited.

ISBN: 1718751850
ISBN-13: 9781718751859

CONTENTS

Introduction i

Chapter one: Introduction To Ethereum 1

Chapter Two: How Ethereum Works 12

Chapter Three: Understanding Gas 26

Chapter Four: How To Buy Ether 33

Chapter Five: Everything You Need To Know About Ethereum Wallets 45

Chapter Six: Security Best Practices To Keep Your Ether Safe 61

Chapter Seven: Ethereum Mining 69

Chapter Eight: Investing In Ethereum 81

Final Words 100

Introduction

Imagine making a modest investment and then sitting back and watching as your investment turns into millions of dollars. Is that even possible? With Ethereum, it is.

Up until recently, Bitcoin was the unchallenged king of the crypto jungle. However, the dominance of Bitcoin has been shaken and is being threatened by Ethereum, the second largest cryptocurrency by market cap, one whose vision is to become a global super computer. Since its invention, the price of Ethereum has grown by over 45,800%, turning every day Joes into overnight millionaires and billionaires. The good thing is that you can also turn your investment into a fortune by investing in Ethereum.

In this book, you are going to learn everything you need to know about Ethereum. You will learn what Ethereum is, how it works, how to mine Ethereum and how to keep your Ether safe, as well as how to invest in Ethereum. After completing this book, you will be ready to step out into the crypto markets and start investing in Ethereum with confidence.

Are you ready to learn about a new technology that will change the world and how you can make money from it? Let's dive in..

Chapter one: Introduction To Ethereum

In this chapter, you are going to learn what Ethereum is, the differences between Ethereum and Bitcoin, the history of Ethereum, its advantages and disadvantages as well as some of its real life use cases.

If you have even been remotely interested in the crypto scene, you have definitely heard about Ethereum. After Bitcoin, Ethereum is the world's largest cryptocurrency by market cap, and is hailed as the cryptocurrency that will bring mainstream adoption of blockchain technology. Despite being so huge and holding so much promise, many people beyond the nerdy world of programmers and computer wizards do not really understand what Ethereum is or how it works.

So, what is Ethereum?

Ethereum can be defined as an open source and decentralized software platform on which blockchain-based decentralized applications and smart contracts can be built and deployed. The Ethereum platform also allows other cryptocurrencies to be built on top of it. Before the development of Ethereum, building blockchain-based applications was no small task. It required lots of resources and advanced knowledge in cryptography, programming and mathematics. Ethereum was created as a way to make it easier and faster for developers to build such apps without having to start from scratch. In some circles, Ethereum is described as a decentralized super computer which can be used to build and deploy decentralized apps.

Before we move any further, I want to make it clear that there is a difference between Ethereum and Ether. Ethereum is the entire network or platform, while Ether refers to the tokens that are native to the Ethereum platform. Ether works as fuel within the Ethereum platform. For someone to build and deploy decentralized apps within the Ethereum network, they need Ether. Miners who keep the Ethereum network running are also rewarded in Ether for their efforts. Since they are tokens, Ether can be bought and sold on cryptocurrency exchanges. Therefore, when someone says that they own some Ethereum, what they actually mean is that they own some Ether.

Ethereum Vs. Bitcoin

To make it easier to understand Ethereum, we are going to compare it to Bitcoin. Since it is the world's first, largest and most popular cryptocurrency, many people have some basic knowledge of how Bitcoin works.

Bitcoin and Ethereum are both decentralized and distributed public blockchain networks. Decentralization means that both networks are not controlled by any central authority. Since they are distributed networks, they exists simultaneously on all the computers (nodes) that form part of the network. They are public, meaning that everyone can access the transactions recorded within either blockchain network.

The greatest difference between Ethereum and Bitcoin lies in their functionality. Bitcoin was specifically built to be an online payment system. The Bitcoin blockchain is simply designed to record and monitor the ownership of units of cryptocurrency (Bitcoins). However, this is only one application of blockchain technology. Blockchain technology can be used for so much more. By allowing blockchain-based decentralized applications to be built and run on top of it, Ethereum expands the capabilities of blockchain technology. Unlike Bitcoin, Ethereum was not built to be a payment system. The aim is to allow autonomous programs to be written on it. These programs can then execute automatically without the need for human intervention. There's no limit to the number or kind of decentralized applications that can be built on the Ethereum network. The only limit lies in the developer's imagination and creativity.

To make it even easier to understand, we will compare the two cryptocurrencies to email and the internet. The invention of the internet made the creation of email possible. However, email is only one application of the internet. So much more can be done on the internet. Bitcoin can be compared to email, while Ethereum can be compared to the internet. While Bitcoin is only one application of blockchain technology, Ethereum allows so much more to be achieved using blockchain technology.

Ethereum Vs. Ethereum Classic

One of the most confusing things for people who are new to Ethereum is to learn that there are two versions of the platform: Ethereum (ETH) and Ethereum Classic (ETC). What's the difference between the two? Why do two versions of the platform exist?

Remember, Ethereum is a platform on which decentralized applications can be built and deployed. One of the very first decentralized applications to be built on the Ethereum platform was the Decentralized Autonomous Organization (DAO). The DAO was meant to be a decentralized VC fund that would autonomously invest in crypto projects and earn profits for the investors. The DAO was a great idea, and it garnered a lot of interest from potential investors. When the DAO issued a crowd sale, it raised over $150 million. However, some hackers took advantage of a flaw in the DAO's code and stole more than $50 million worth of Ether from the project.

It's important to note that the thieves hacked the DAO code, not the Ethereum platform itself. However, since the DAO was one of the first and largest decentralized apps being built on the Ethereum platform, the hack had a very negative impact on the Ethereum platform. People assumed that the Ethereum platform was not safe, and the value of Ether and the market cap of Ethereum fell dramatically. In order to recoup the losses incurred by people who had invested in the DAO, there was a proposal to undo the malicious transaction by reverting the Ethereum blockchain to the state it was before the malicious transaction. To do this, a hard fork was implemented on the Ethereum platform to invalidate the theft.

However, not everyone within the Ethereum community was in agreement with the idea to undo the malicious transaction. They believed that no one had the right to change the blockchain, and instead of upgrading to the new blockchain, they continued mining the old version of Ethereum. This led to the creation of two versions of the Ethereum blockchain, with the old version being referred to as Ethereum Classic and the new version retaining the name Ethereum.

After the fork, the two versions of Ethereum continued on their own divergent paths. For instance, the Ethereum Classic team introduced a maximum cap on the number of tokens that will be generated within the lifetime of the platform, something that is non-existent on Ethereum. There are also plans for Ethereum to shift to a proof of stake (PoS) consensus system, while Ethereum Classic has chosen to stick with proof of work (PoW). Currently, Ethereum has a market cap of about $42 billion, while Ethereum Classic has a market cap of about $1 billion.

The History Of Ethereum

Ethereum was envisioned by a 19-year-old Russian-Canadian programmer known as Vitalik Buterin. Vitalik became an early adopter of Bitcoin after learning about it from his father in 2011. After using Bitcoin for a while, Vitalik realized that decentralization brought about by the blockchain technology could be applied to more than just payment systems. Vitalik saw that it was possible to do this by building a programming language into a blockchain. In 2013, he wrote a paper describing the concept of Ethereum. In January 2014, Vitalik made a formal announcement of the Ethereum project at the North American Bitcoin Conference. After receiving $100,000 from the Thiel Fellowship, Vitalik dropped from school to concentrate on the Ethereum project. In April of the same year, the first prototype platform for the Ethereum project was launched. In July 2014, the first Ether sale was held. In August 2014, the Ethereum project issued a presale and raised over $14 million. In 2015, the first milestone of the Ethereum project went live. In 2016, Ethereum gained a lot of media attention after a crowd sale raised over $150 million for the DAO project. However, this attention would soon turn negative after the DAO was hacked about a month later, leading to the loss of about $50 million. In February 2017, Microsoft along with other huge tech firms and major banks came together with the Ethereum team to form the Enterprise Ethereum Alliance, an organization that seeks to spearhead the spread of Ethereum blockchain technology. Such developments have contributed to the view that Ethereum will soon become the largest cryptocurrency.

Advantages And Disadvantages Of Ethereum

Advantages

Ethereum has a number of advantages. These include:

- With the formation of the Enterprise Ethereum Alliance, Ethereum has received lots of backing from the corporate sector, to a level that can only be matched by Bitcoin. This resulted in an upsurge in the price of Ethereum and gives investors the confidence that they are investing in a project that promises longevity.

- Unlike Bitcoin and most other cryptocurrencies, Ethereum allows the development and deployment of all kinds of decentralized apps. This means that there is no limit to the possible real-life applications of the platform.
- Since Ethereum is decentralized, it eliminates the need for third parties and central authorities, making it easier and faster to perform non-trust transactions.
- Ever since its announcement, Ethereum has had an elaborate roadmap, which they have followed religiously. This makes it a good asset to invest in since it has a clear vision and is backed by a team capable of steering it towards the achievement of this vision.
- With other applications being built on the Ethereum platform, a strong ecosystem is gradually growing around the platform. As more and more services are built on the platform, it will attract more and more users, creating a network effect that will push its adoption even further.
- Ethereum is a distributed system that exists simultaneously on thousands of computers all over the world, so it has no central point of failure or vulnerability. This also means that it is not under the control of any one entity.

- By taking advantage of smart contracts, Ethereum is a very reliable platform for issuing crowd sales to fund various projects. This explains why most Initial Coin Offerings (ICOs) are being implemented on the Ethereum network.
- Mining Ether is a lot easier than mining Bitcoin and does not need any specialized ASICs (Application Specific Integrated Circuits). Instead, you can still mine Ether using a GPU.

Disadvantages

- Since Ethereum is a platform on which other applications should be built, its strength lies in the applications that will be built on it. Failure to develop useful decentralized apps on Ethereum kills the value of Ethereum.
- Ethereum is still a relatively new technology, therefore there are only a handful of developers who are well versed with creating blockchain-based DApps and smart contracts. Learning from scratch is also difficult since there is not enough documentation available about coding for Ethereum. However, as the Ethereum community continues growing, more documentation will be available.
- Since Ethereum is designed to be flexible, it cannot achieve the same level of effectiveness

as blockchains that are specifically built for one single task, such as Bitcoin.
- Ethereum is an online system, therefore any decentralized apps built on the platform cannot be used without internet access.

Chapter Summary

In this chapter, you have learned:

- Ethereum is an open source and decentralized software platform on which blockchain-based decentralized applications and smart contracts can be built and deployed.
- Ethereum is the entire network or platform, while Ether refers to the tokens that are native to the Ethereum platform.
- The Bitcoin blockchain is simply designed to record and monitor the ownership of units of cryptocurrency, which is only one application of blockchain technology.
- By allowing blockchain-based decentralized applications to be built and run on top of it, Ethereum expands the capabilities of blockchain technology.
- There are two versions of the Ethereum blockchain – Ethereum and Ethereum Classic. Ethereum

Classic is the older version, while Ethereum is the new blockchain that was formed following the hard fork that happened after The DAO hack.
- Ethereum was invented in 2014 by Vitalik Buterin, a young Russian Canadian programmer.
- Ethereum is the only major cryptocurrency that supports smart contracts.

In the next chapter, you will learn how Ethereum works.

Chapter Two: How Ethereum Works

In this chapter, you are going to learn how the Ethereum network works and how concepts like smart contracts, DAOs and DApps (decentralized applications) function on the network.

Just like Bitcoin, the Ethereum network is based on a shared and immutable public ledger. This ledger is distributed among all the computers (nodes) that form part of the network. Each node holds the most recent version of the blockchain, constantly checking in with other nodes to ensure that it updates its copy to reflect any changes made on the blockchain.

However, there is a major difference between the two blockchains. The Bitcoin blockchain simply keeps a record of all Bitcoin transactions. Since Ethereum is like a huge distributed super computer on which other applications can be run, it must not only keep a record of all Ether transactions, it also needs to keep track of the latest states of all the applications running on it and the smart contracts built on it, their addresses and the unique conditions that determine the execution of the smart contract.

Smart Contracts

I have mentioned the term smart contract severely so far, and you might be wondering what they are. Smart contracts are a new form of transaction protocol that was made possible by the invention of blockchain technology. In their simplest form, smart contracts are basically contracts that can execute themselves without the need for human intervention. They are computer programs that set out the terms of a contract and that automatically and autonomously execute these terms once certain pre-defined conditions are met. Instead of being enforceable by law as traditional contracts, smart contracts are enforced by computer code. Below are some properties of smart contracts:

- Smart contracts are built and executed on the blockchain.
- The execution of smart contracts is determined and verified by computer code.
- The execution of smart contracts leads to a change in the state of the blockchain.

Where Did They Originate?

Though smart contracts have only started being implemented just recently, they are not an entirely new phenomenon. The idea of a smart contract was first conceptualized in the early 1990's by Nick Szabo, a cryptographer and programmer who also made great contributions to the development of cryptocurrencies. Despite having conceptualized the idea, Nick Szabo was unable to implement his idea because smart contracts had to be deployed on a blockchain, which had not been invented at the time. The implementation of smart contracts became possible with the invention of blockchain technology by Satoshi Nakamoto, Bitcoin's mysterious inventor. Bitcoin was the first cryptocurrency to use smart contracts. However, the smart contracts used in Bitcoin are very limited. They can only handle conditions that are related to payment transactions. The development of Ethereum expanded the capabilities of smart contracts, making it possible for them to be customized and deployed on all sorts of transactions.

Are They Really Necessary?

Before looking at the importance of smart contracts, we should first consider the role played by traditional contracts. Contracts emerged as a way for people who do not trust each other to transact with each other. They are a way for the parties involved in the transaction to protect themselves from being cheated or defrauded. For instance, before you do some work for a client, it is the norm for both of you to sign a contract showing the agreement between the two of you. This way, if one of you does not fulfill his part, the contract acts as proof of your agreement, which can be enforced by law.

On this front, smart contracts are not any different from traditional contracts. Their role is to allow transactions to be carried out between two parties in the absence of trust. However, the enforcement of smart contracts is a bit different from that of traditional contracts. For instance, let's look at our previous example where you signed a traditional agreement before commencing work for a client. Sometimes, the client might fail to pay your dues after you have provided your services. In this instance, your only recourse would be to go to a court of law, which would then order the client to hold their end of the deal or risk being fined or sent to jail. This means time wasted and extra expenses for the legal fees. With smart contracts, there is no risk of non-compliance. Once the predetermined conditions are met (provision of services), the smart contract automatically and autonomously executes the terms (payment for service rendered) as stipulated within the contract.

How Do They Work?

Like most computer programs, smart contracts use an 'IF/THEN' logic. If a certain condition is met, then a certain action takes place. For instance, in the above example, the terms of the contract would be IF service is provided, THEN payment gets released to service provider. Remember, I mentioned that smart contracts can be customized for any kind of transaction. This means that you can include as many IF/THEN conditions as necessary as part of a smart contract.

For a smart contract to be set up, there are a number of things that have to be done. The first one is the definition and submission of the subject of the contract. The smart contract needs access to whatever is being transacted under the contract. In our example, the subject of the contract would be the payment being made by your client. This allows the smart contract to lock the payment (subject) until you meet the conditions of the contract, at which point it will automatically release the payment to you. Secondly, there is need to define the terms of the contract. These are the conditions that will trigger the automatic execution of the smart contract. In our case, the terms would be the service your client has hired you to provide. Once the terms are defined, both parties must sign the contract with their digital signatures. Just like traditional contracts, a smart contract does not become valid until it is signed by all the involved parties. However, unlike the traditional contract which you sign with your pen or official stamp/seal, a smart contract is signed using your private key, which controls the access to your digital wallet.

Advantages Of Smart Contracts

Smart contracts have several advantages over traditional contracts, which include:

- **Autonomy** – One of the biggest advantages of smart contracts is that they are self-executing. This eliminates the need for third parties, such as lawyers and courts, and the fees and time resources needed for intervention by these third parties. Smart contracts also eliminate the risk of the third party being corrupted to change the terms of the contract.
- **Trust** – This is related to the previous point. Since the smart contract is autonomous, you can take part in non-trust-based transactions with the confidence that all parties will hold their end of the deal.
- **Safety** – If you were to lose your copy of a traditional contract, then you have no way of proving that you actually entered into a contract with the other party. Smart contracts, on the other hand, are stored on the blockchain, which is permanent and immutable. This means that your contract is as safe as can be.

DAOs And Decentralized Apps (DApps)

Apart from smart contracts, there are two other new technologies that are closely tied to the Ethereum network. These are DAO's and DApps. These two concepts can be a bit confusing for beginners. This is because, on the surface, they appear to be similar. However, they are not one and the same thing. In this section, let us take a look at the differences between DAO's and DApps.

Decentralized Autonomous Organizations (DAO's)

Before we get to the actual definition of DAO's, let us look at a thought experiment that was introduced in 2009 by Mike Hearn, a former Bitcoin contributor. In the thought experiment, picture a self-driving cab that drives around the city looking for passengers. At the end of every day, it uses the profits earned from the day's work to refuel itself and to automatically pay for its insurance. Every Saturday morning, it drives itself to the mechanic for servicing. All this happens without human intervention. Does this sound unbelievable? This is the kind of revolution set to be brought about by DAO's.

Also known as Decentralized Autonomous Corporations (DAC's), these are organizations that run autonomously by following conditions prescribed by smart contracts. All the rules governing the operation of the organization are encoded into smart contracts and put on the blockchain. This eliminates the need for hierarchical management to enforce the rules of the organization. In other words, a DAO is similar to a normal company, only that the DAO operates on the blockchain environment, with the organization's rules being enforced by smart contracts. The idea of DAO's came about after people in the crypto space realized that blockchain technology could do away with managerial wastage the same way Bitcoin made it possible to do away with middlemen in the financial sector.

It is important to note that there is a difference between DAO and The DAO. DAO represents the type of blockchain-based leaderless organizations, while The DAO (the one that got hacked) was the name of one of the first organizations of this kind.

So, if there is no management in DAO's, how are decisions made within the organization? Since the DAO is decentralized, the power to make decisions is devolved to all members of the organization. Any member of the organization is allowed to make a proposal. The rest of the members in the organization then vote in favor of or against the proposal and the decision is made based on consensus. In the normal world, such a decision-making structure would be tiring and time consuming. However, since this happens on the blockchain, with the members of the organization being represented by computers, decisions can be made much faster.

DAO's make it possible for people from all over the world to work together towards a common objective without the need for third parties to instill trust. While this is nothing new, DAO's offer a faster and more efficient way of doing it, similar to how smart contracts are more efficient than traditional contracts.

Anyone can invest in or take part in a DAO. All you need is to have a wallet and be well versed with the process of purchasing Bitcoins or Ether (this will be discussed in greater detail in Chapter Four). To invest in a DAO, you simply need to purchase the tokens related to that DAO. The tokens act as shares, giving you a right to vote on the affairs of the DAO or a claim of the profits made by the DAO. Similar to owning shares, the more the tokens you own, the more voting power you have.

Advantages Of DAO's

Since the aim of DAO's is to make the running and operation of ordinary organizations more efficient, DAO's have a number of advantages. These include:

- Decision making is based on consensus and all the members of the organization have the opportunity to make their contribution towards the running of the organization.

- The lack of hierarchical structure means that any member can put forward their proposal for consideration by the entire organization.
- The rules governing the operation of the DAO are pre-written and cannot be changed, which eliminates the risk of the goals and objectives of the organization being corrupted.
- DAO's are transparent, since all the rules and financial transactions are permanently and immutably recorded on the blockchain, which is accessible to all members of the organization.
- In order for a member to put forward a proposal, they need to spend some tokens. This incentivizes the members to think through their decisions and keeps the organization from being spammed with ineffective solutions.

Disadvantages of DAO's

- Since they are a relatively new concept, DAOs have not been fully tried and tested.
- Since DAO's are essentially based on code, any errors or bugs within the code can be exploited by people with malicious intentions, such as was the case with The DAO hack.
- DAO's devolve decision making power to the masses. Some experts feel that this is not a very wise move, especially in financial matters.

- In order for DAO's to gain mainstream adoption in the real world, there is need for legal frameworks to govern their operation, something that is non-existent at the moment.

Decentralized Applications (DApps)

Decentralized applications are still a fairly recent concept, so there is no unanimous definition that can be used to describe them. They are a new breed of apps that cannot be stopped, that have no downtime and that are not owned by any one person. Despite the lack of a unanimously accepted definition of 'decentralized applications', there are certain properties that any application must have before it is categorized as a DApp. For an application to be considered as a DApp, it needs to be open source, it has to be built on top of a public and decentralized blockchain, it needs to use tokens that are cryptographically generated, and it needs to have an inbuilt protocol for ensuring consensus.

Sometimes, decentralized apps are confused with smart contracts. To understand the difference between DApps and smart contracts, we can compare DApps to websites that are blockchain enabled, while smart contracts are the technology that allow these websites to access the blockchain. In a normal, traditional website, the front end of the website (what you see) uses API's to connect to the database containing the files that make up the website. With DApps (blockchain enabled website), the front end of the website uses a smart contract to connect to a blockchain. This means that smart contracts are a part of DApps.

Another major difference between DApps and traditional applications is that traditional applications are hosted on centralized servers. This means that if the server fails, then a traditional application would experience some downtime. DApps, on the other hand, are hosted on decentralized peer to peer networks. This means that it is impossible for the DApp to experience downtime, since it is practically impossible for the entire network to fail simultaneously.

Chapter Summary

In this chapter, you have learned:

- Smart contracts are basically contracts that can execute themselves without the need for human intervention. They automatically and autonomously execute these terms once certain pre-defined conditions are met.
- Smart contracts were first conceptualized in the early 1990's by Nick Szabo.
- Bitcoin was the first cryptocurrency to use smart contracts, though the smart contracts used in Bitcoin are very limited.

- The development of Ethereum expanded the capabilities of smart contracts, making it possible for them to be customized and deployed on all sorts of transactions.
- Smart contracts are similar to traditional contracts, only that they are executed on and enforced by the blockchain. This makes them more effective and efficient.
- Smart contracts use an 'IF/THEN' logic. If a certain condition is met, then a certain action takes place.
- For smart contracts to work, they require a subject, the terms of the contract, and the digital signatures of the parties involved.
- Smart contracts provide autonomy, trust and safety.
- Decentralized Autonomous Organizations (DAO's) are organizations that run autonomously by following conditions prescribed by smart contracts.
- A DAO is similar to a normal company, only that the DAO operates on the blockchain environment, with the organization's rules being enforced by smart contracts.
- Since the DAO is decentralized, the power to make decisions is devolved to all members of the organization.

- Decentralized applications (DApps) are a new breed of apps that cannot be stopped, that have no downtime and that are not owned by anyone.
- For an application to be considered as a DApp, it needs to be open source, it has to be built on top of a public and decentralized blockchain, it needs to use tokens that are cryptographically generated, and it needs to have an inbuilt protocol for ensuring consensus.
- Since DApps are run on decentralized peer to peer networks, they cannot suffer downtimes resulting from server failures.

In the next chapter, you are going to learn about gas and its role within the Ethereum network.

Chapter Three: Understanding Gas

In this chapter, you are going to learn about what gas is and how it works.

The Ethereum network brought with it several new concepts that do not exist on other cryptocurrency networks. One of these is something known as gas. This is something that most people have a hard time understanding. Whenever you want to make a transaction on the Ethereum network, you will notice that you will be prompted to enter a gas price and gas limit (some wallets automatically decide on the gas price and gas limit to keep things simpler for users).

So, what it this gas, and how does it work?

Whenever you perform an operation on the Ethereum network, whether it is sending Ether or interacting with a smart contract, some computations will have to be performed by miners on the Ethereum network for your operation to be successful. For their work, the miners need to be paid. This is where gas comes in. Gas is a unit that is used to measure the amount of work (computation) that had to be done for your transaction to go through. However, the payment for the transaction is paid in Ether.

To make this concept easier to understand, let us compare it to using electricity in your house. Whenever you wash your clothes in the washing machine, the machine uses electricity, which you need to pay for. You can think of the electricity as the computational resources needed for Ethereum operations. However, the electricity used up as you do your laundry is not measured in dollars. It is measured in Kilowatts per hour. Similarly, the amount of computational resources needed in order for your Ethereum transaction to go through are measured in gas, instead of Ether. Finally, despite being measured in kilowatts per hour, you pay for your electricity consumption in dollars. The same way, despite being measured in gas, you pay for the amount of computation done for your operation to go through in Ether, not gas.

Every operation on the Ethereum network requires gas. However, different operations require different amounts of gas, depending on the amount of computation that must be done for the computation to go through. Simple operations like sending Ether need only some little gas, while more complex operations like interacting with multiple smart contracts need higher amounts of gas.

You might be wondering why the payment for transactions is measured in terms of gas instead of simply charging a certain amount of Ether per operation. Ether is a token that is publicly traded on cryptocurrency exchanges, therefore the value of Ether is subject to rapid market fluctuations. At the same time, the amount of computational resources required for transactions does not change as rapidly. This means that a 20x increase in the price of Ether would lead to a 20x increase in the amount paid for the same transaction. This is not very sustainable. The gas system was therefore created as a solution to keep the computation fees independent from the price of Ether.

Gas Limit

Before performing any operation on the Ethereum network, you will be required to set the gas limit for your transaction. This determines the highest amount of gas you are willing to spend on the operation. Gas limit is a precautionary mechanism that keeps you from using up all your Ether in a faulty operation. For instance, if you execute a smart contract that has a bug, it would keep running without achieving the desired objective. However, since it is still running, it still requires computational resources, so you would keep paying for an operation that is not going anywhere. However, by setting a gas limit, the faulty operation will only continue until runs out of gas, at which point it will stop.

The recommended gas limit for standard transactions is 21000. If you set the gas limit for your transaction as 50000 and your transaction only uses up only 21000, all the extra gas will be refunded to you once the transaction is complete. Even though it is up to you to set your preferred gas limit, you cannot lower your transaction cost by lowering your gas limit. The amount of gas required for a transaction depends on the amount of code that must be executed in order for the transaction to go through. Therefore, it is not up to you to determine how much gas the transaction will use up. If you set too low a gas limit, the transaction will run out of gas without being completed. The used-up gas won't be refunded to you. Instead, it will be kept by the miner, since they have already spent their computational resources executing your operation.

Gas Price

Apart from setting the gas limit, Ethereum transactions will also require you to set the amount you are willing to spend for gas. Gas price is usually measured in Gwei, which is a fraction of an Ether to the 9th decimal place. The ability to determine your gas price means that you can lower your transaction cost by entering a lower gas price. However, the system is made in such a way that it encourages people to use a reasonable gas price. The gas price you decide to pay for your transaction determines how fast your transaction will be mined. How does this work?

For every transaction on the Ethereum transaction, the transaction fees are paid to the miner who provide the computational resources for the transaction. Whenever you initiate a transaction, it is entered into a pool from which miners then pick transactions to include in a block. It is up to the miner to decide which transactions to include in the block. As such, it is only logical that they will first choose the transactions with a high gas price since they get the highest returns from processing these transactions. Therefore, if your transaction has a high gas price, the high gas price will be an incentive for miners to process your transactions before those with a low gas price. If you set a gas price that is too low, no miner will be willing to add it to a block, so it will remain as a pending transaction. This means that you should set a gas price that is high enough for miners to want to include it in a block. If you need your transaction to be processed faster, you can set a higher gas price. The actual transaction cost for a transaction (paid in Ether) is a factor of the number of units of gas used for the transaction and the transaction's gas price.

Chapter Summary

In this chapter, you have learned:

- Gas is a unit that is used to measure the amount of computation that had to be done in order for your transaction to go through.
- Though transaction costs are calculated in terms of gas, the payment for the transaction is paid in Ether.
- Different operations on the Ethereum blockchain require different amounts of gas, depending on the amount of computation that must be done for the computation to go through.
- The gas system was created as a solution to keep the computation fees independent from the price of Ether.
- The gas limit determines the highest amount of gas you are willing to spend on an operation on the Ethereum blockchain.
- Gas limit is a precautionary mechanism that keeps you from using up all your Ether in a faulty operation.
- Gas price is the amount of Ether you are willing to for gas.
- The gas price you decide to pay for your transaction determines how fast your transaction will be mined.

- The actual cost for a transaction on the Ethereum blockchain is a factor of the number of units of gas used for the transaction and the transaction's gas price.

In the next chapter, you will learn how to buy Ether.

Chapter Four: How To Buy Ether

In this chapter, you are going to learn various methods through which you can buy Ether, and how to go about using each of these methods. Keep in mind that before you get started on the process of buying Ether, you first need to get yourself an Ethereum wallet, you can go with any of the options discussed in Chapter Five.

The simplest and most straightforward method of buying Ether is to go through a cryptocurrency exchange. These are online platforms that facilitate the trading of cryptocurrencies between users. Owing to Ethereum's popularity and huge market cap, there are several cryptocurrency exchanges that support Ether, which means you have multiple options regardless of your location. While different cryptocurrency exchanges have slightly different procedures, the process is of buying Ether through a cryptocurrency exchange involves the following:

The first thing you need to do is to create an account with your exchange of choice. This step will involve providing some information about yourself, such as your name and email address. Before signing up for an account, it is important to confirm that the exchange has support for your country and the fiat currency you intend to use to purchase Ether.

Once you have signed up for an account, most exchanges will require you to provide some additional information before you can make deposits or withdrawals. In most cases, they will ask for your government issued identification, a photo of yourself and a proof of address. This is done to ensure that the exchange is in compliance with Anti-Money Laundering (AML) and Know Your Customer (KYC) laws.

Now that you have verified your identity and address, you can go ahead and choose your preferred deposit method. Different exchanges accept different deposit methods, so you need to check this before signing up for the account. This information can easily be found on the exchange's website, along with the fees charged for each method. Some of the most common deposit methods supported include wire transfers, PayPal payments, SEPA and credit/debit cards.

Once you identify the deposit method that works best for you, you can now go ahead and deposit your fiat currency into the exchange platform. Dollars and Euros are supported on almost every exchange, while many other exchanges support other major fiat currencies such as Sterling Pounds, Canadian Dollars, Japanese Yen and Chinese Yuan. Your deposit might take anywhere between a couple of hours to a few days to reflect in your exchange platform account, depending on your chosen deposit method.

Once your funds reflect in your exchange platform account, you are ready to buy Ether. The process varies depending on your chosen exchange, though most exchanges try to keep the process simple and intuitive, even for beginners. After receiving the Ether in your exchange platform account, it is always advisable to transfer them to a wallet whose keys *you* control. Do not leave them on the exchange platform.

Popular Cryptocurrency Exchanges Where You Can Buy Ether

Coinbase

This is the world's most popular cryptocurrency exchange, and a good option for you if you want to buy some Ether from the USA, Canada, the UK, Europe and Singapore. In addition to Ether, Coinbase supports several other cryptocurrencies. Coinbase has been in operation for over six years and has established itself as one of the most reliable and trustworthy exchanges. Buying Ether through Coinbase is easy and straightforward. If you are a more experienced user, you can also use Coinbase's GDAX, which offers a more advanced set of features. Coinbase allows users to deposit funds (fiat currency) through bank transfers, SEPA and credit/debit cards. However, if you opt to use credit/debit card payments, you will have to contend with a much lower limit. Despite being the most popular cryptocurrency exchange, Coinbase is only available in 32 countries. Therefore, you need too ascertain that your country is supported before signing up. It's also good to note that Coinbase does not sell Ethereum Classic.

CEX.io

This is another popular exchange that that has been around for a while. The platform is registered with Fincen and provides brokerage services in addition to being a crypto exchange. Cex.io started supporting Ethereum in 2016 after they brought their cloud mining service to an end. Unlike Coinbase, Cex.io is available worldwide. You can deposit your funds on Cex.io through wire transfers, SEPA or credit/debit card. Getting verified gives allows you to buy a higher amount of Ether through credit card. The Cex.io website is intuitive and user-friendly, which makes the buying process quite easy, even for beginners. On the flip side, the fees charged by Cex.io are a bit on the higher side.

However, it is still a good option for those who live in countries not supported by Coinbase.

Coinmama

Founded in 2013, Coinmama is a cryptocurrency exchange and brokerage service that supports Bitcoin and Ethereum. One of the greatest advantages of Coinmama is that you can buy up to $125 worth of Ether without being verified. This means you can go to their website, sign up, and complete your purchase in less than 20 minutes. Coinmama only allows you to buy Ethereum using credit or debit card. Their customer support is quite excellent, and the service is available worldwide. However, their fees are a bit high.

BitPanda

Formerly known as Coinimal, BitPanda is an Austrian cryptocurrency broker that allows people within the Eurozone to buy and sell Ether. Founded in 2014, the platform has gained a lot of popularity among users in Europe. BitPanda allows you to pay for Ether through SEPA, credit card, Skrill and several other payment methods that are popular in Europe. Their fees are fairly low, and their website is quite fast and secure

Gemini

Founded in 2015 by the Winklevoss twins, the New York based cryptocurrency exchange has rapidly grown in popularity. Gemini offers its services to users in North America, Europe and Asia. The Gemini platform works like a traditional forex exchange, allowing users to trade with each other directly, with prices being determined by the users. Gemini only supports deposits made through bank transfer. One of its greatest advantages is that its fees are low.

Changelly

Founded in 2016, Changelly is still a fairly new entrant into the market. Despite having not been around for long, it has also become quite popular. One of the best features of Changelly is that it allows users to trade one cryptocurrency for another. This makes the platform a good option if you already own some Bitcoin that you want to exchange for Ether. While it is possible to buy Ethereum from Changelly using fiat currency, the fees are quite high. If you have some Bitcoin that you want to exchange for Ether, the process will take you about 30 minutes.

Bitfinex

Bitfinex is a Bitcoin exchange that also allows users to trade cryptocurrency pairs. This means that, if you own some Bitcoin, you can exchange it for Ether on the platform. Bitfinex does not support fiat currency, therefore the only way of acquiring Ether through the platform is to buy some Bitcoin first. Bitfinex is quite secure, with advanced security mechanisms to keep customer information safe. Users' funds are also stored in cold wallets to eliminate the threat of online hacking attacks.

Kraken

This is another US based cryptocurrency exchange that allows you to buy Ether using fiat currency or in exchange for other cryptocurrencies. Kraken is one of the very first exchanges to be established, having been founded in 2011. Kraken supports more cryptocurrency pairs than Gemini and Coinbase. If you decide to buy Ether from Kraken using fiat currency, you can make deposits through bank transfer. The only complaint about Kraken is that their user interface is poor. Their customer support is also said to be a bit slow.

Purchasing Ethereum Anonymously

Like I mentioned earlier, purchasing Ether through an online exchange will require you to provide proof of your identity. However, sometimes you might want to purchase Ether anonymously for one reason or the other. In this case, you can do so by purchasing Ether from peer to peer exchange platforms, such as localethereum.com.

Localethereum.com is a platform that brings together Ethereum buyers and sellers within the same geographical region. You can think of it as an online marketplace, just like eBay, only that the product in this case is Ether. The buyer and seller can agree on a payment method that works best for both of them whether that is bank transfer, PayPal, Skrill, credit card, Bitcoin, or even cash. For its efforts, localethereum.com charges the seller a small percentage of the trade. This is the most effective method of buying Ether anonymously. However, you might need to take some precautions. For instance, if you decide to meet up with the seller to exchange Ether for cash, you need to think about your own personal safety.

Alternatively, you can purchase Bitcoin and then exchange your Bitcoin for ether on shapeshift.io. This is an exchange that allows you to exchange different cryptocurrencies without having to create an account with the platform. However, you cannot buy a large amount of Ether from shapeshift.io.

Finally, you can purchase Ether anonymously from an Ethereum ATM. These are ATM machines that allow you to exchange cash for Ether. Ethereum ATM's do not require any form of identification. All you need to do is to select the amount of Ether you want, enter your Ethereum wallet address and insert money into the machine. The Ether will be automatically sent to your wallet. However, since Ethereum ATM's do not ask for proof of identity, you can only buy small amounts of Ether from an Ethereum ATM.

How To Choose The Best Ethereum Exchange

With so many available options, choosing the best Ethereum exchange for your needs can be a bit hectic. To ensure that you are making the right decision, below are some factors you should consider before settling on a specific exchange platform.

Supported location: Some exchanges like Coinbase and Gemini only offer their services in specific geographical regions. Therefore, before registering for an account with an exchange platform, you need to ensure that their services are available in your geographical location.

Deposit methods: You also need to confirm whether an exchange supports you preferred deposit method. For instance, if you want to make your deposit via PayPal, you cannot use Gemini. You should also keep in mind that different deposit methods attract different fees. Generally, the faster and more convenient the deposit method, the higher the amount of fees you can expect to pay.

Supported currency: Different exchanges accept deposits in different currencies. In most cases, this depends on location. Most exchanges accept USD and Euro deposits. However, if you intend to use any other currency, it is always good to first check whether the currency is accepted on your preferred exchange. For instance, if you intend to deposit Japanese Yen, you can only use an exchange that accepts Japanese Yen deposits. Similarly, you cannot use Bitfinex if you intend to buy Ether using fiat currency.

Security: Buying Ether involves money therefore you need to be sure that you can entrust your funds and personal/financial information without the risk that it might get stolen by hackers. Check the exchange's website to find out the kind of security measures they have in place to protect your funds and information.

Support: Sometimes, you might face some challenges setting up your account or buying Ether, especially if you are a beginner. You want an exchange that has a responsive and helpful support who will quickly help you solve any issues that might arise.

Fees: Different cryptocurrency exchanges have different fee structures. You should look for one that offers you the lowest fees.

Reputation: Finally, before settling on a specific exchange, it is always a good idea to check its reputation. What are other people saying about it? Check different online forums and review websites to see the kind of reputation the exchange platform has. If you come across several customer complaints, this should act as a red flag.

The above are some of the considerations you should have in mind when choosing a cryptocurrency exchange. However, sometimes it is impossible to find one that meets all your requirements. In such instances, you might have to sacrifice on some of these factors. For instance, if the only exchange supported in your country charges high fees, you might have no other option but to go with it or forego buying Ether.

Chapter Summary

In this chapter, you have learned:

- The simplest and most straightforward method of buying Ether is to go through a cryptocurrency exchange.
- Most cryptocurrency exchange platforms will ask for your government issued identification, a photo of yourself and a proof of address in order to remain in compliance with Anti-Money

Laundering (AML) and Know Your Customer (KYC) laws.
- Different exchanges accept different deposit methods, so you need to check this before signing up for an account with a cryptocurrency exchange.
- After receiving Ether in your exchange platform account, it is always advisable to transfer them to a wallet whose keys you control. Do not leave them on the exchange platform.
- Some popular cryptocurrency exchanges where you can buy Ether include Coinbase, CEX.io, Coinmama, BitPanda, Changelly, Gemini, Bitfinex and Kraken.
- If you want to purchase Ethereum anonymously, you can do so by purchasing Ether from peer to peer exchange platforms, such as localethereum.com. You can also purchase Bitcoin and then exchange your Bitcoin for Ether on shapeshift.io.
- You can also purchase Ether anonymously from an Ethereum ATM.
- To choose the best Ethereum exchange, you should consider factors such as supported location, supported deposit methods, supported currencies, security, fees, customer support and reputation.

In the next chapter, you will learn about Ethereum wallets.

Chapter Five: Everything You Need To Know About Ethereum Wallets

In this chapter, you are going to learn about what Ethereum wallets are, how to choose the right Ethereum wallet for your needs, the different types of Ethereum wallets and the characteristics of a good Ethereum wallet.

In the previous chapter, I mentioned that before you go about the process of purchasing Ether, you need to get yourself an Ethereum wallet. So, what is an Ethereum wallet? If I give you a hundred-dollar bill, you will most likely put it inside a wallet or purse. The same way you store fiat money in a wallet, you also need a wallet to store digital currency. However, the Ethereum wallet does not look anything like your normal wallet. An Ethereum wallet is basically a piece of software that allows you to access your Ether, monitor your balance and conduct transactions.

Even though I compared an Ethereum wallet to an ordinary, physical wallet, the concept behind an Ethereum wallet is very different from an ordinary wallet. This is because your Ethereum wallet does not actually store any Ether, because Ether does not actually 'exist' per se. Instead, Ether exists as a record of transactions on the blockchain. I know this might sound confusing. To make it easier to understand this, let's look at what happens with fiat currency. If I transfer $1000 from my bank account to your bank account, the $1000 is subtracted from my account and credited to your account. When you check your account balance, you will see the $1000. However, if I send 100 Ether to your wallet, no actual Ether are transferred. Instead, the transfer is a record of transaction inputs and outputs showing that I have signed over the ability to spend 100 ETH to you. I therefore cannot spend the 100 ETH again. If you go ahead and send 50 ETH to someone else, the transaction basically tells the blockchain that you have signed off the ability to spend the 50 ETH to another person.

From the above explanation, it becomes easier to understand what I mean when I say that your Ethereum wallet does not store any Ether. Instead, your wallet simply reads through the record of transactions on the blockchain and determines how many Ether you have permission to spend. Ethereum wallets consist of a pair of two mathematically linked strings of characters. One of these strings is the public key, which is also referred to as your wallet address. When you buy Ether, you must provide the seller with your wallet address. When the seller transfers the Ether to you, they are basically signing off the ability to spend those Ether to that particular public key.

However, for you to spend the Ether signed off to that public key, you need to provide proof that the public key belongs to you. This is where the private key comes in. The private key is what shows that you have the permission to access the Ether and sign them off to another person. If someone gains access to your private key, it means that they can spend your coins. Therefore, instead of Ether, it is your private key that is actually stored within your wallet, giving you the ability to access and spend the Ether. When you say that you have some Ether in your wallet, it actually means that you have access to a public key to which a certain amount of Ether was sent, as well as the corresponding private key that allows you to spend these Ether.

Choosing An Ethereum Wallet

When choosing a wallet to keep your Ether, there are some considerations you need to keep in mind. These include:

Personal Or Third-Party Wallet?

When it comes to storing your Ether, you can go with a third-party wallet provider or opt to create your own wallet. Third party wallets are easy to set up and very convenient. A good example is the wallet provided by your cryptocurrency exchange. However, convenience does not mean that they are the best. Some third-party wallets store your private key for you, which means that they are the ones with full control over your Ether. However, some third-party wallets will allow you to store your private key yourself. If you want absolute control over your Ether, you should create your own Ethereum wallet. However, setting up a personal wallet is a lot more complicated than using a third-party wallet.

Full Node Or Light Client?

Ethereum wallets come either as full nodes or light clients. Full node wallets provide you with direct access to the blockchain. Full node wallets form part of the Ethereum network and are involved in verifying the legitimacy of transactions within the blockchain. This means that a full node will use some of your computers processing power to maintain the blockchain. You can also use them for mining. However, this means that the wallet will have to download the entire blockchain, which can be quite huge. This also means that means full node wallets can only be used on desktop.

If you don't want to expend your processing power to maintain the Ethereum blockchain, you can always use a light wallet. However, since they cannot access the blockchain directly, light clients must connect to another node for them to access the blockchain.

Hot or Cold Wallet?

All kinds of Ethereum wallets can be classified as either hot or cold. Hot wallets are those that store your keys on the internet. This gives you access to your Ether from any part of the world, provided you have access to the internet. While hot wallets are convenient, they are also susceptible to hacking attacks. Cold wallets, on the other hand, keep your Ether more secure by storing your keys offline, where there is no risk of theft by hackers. However, this makes them a lot less convenient. As a rule of thumb, if you intend to store only small amounts of Ether and intend to transact regularly, you can go with a hot wallet. However, if you intend to store large amounts of Ether and do not need to make regular transactions, your best option is a cold wallet.

Types of Ethereum Wallets

Paper Wallets

If you are looking for a simple but safe method of storing your Ether, using a paper wallet is a great option. Remember, I said that the work of an Ethereum wallet is to store your private key. As such, a paper wallet is simply a piece of paper with your private key printed on it. Since the paper wallet does not store your private key digitally, it totally eliminates the threat of your Ether getting stolen by hackers. However, you should remember that your paper wallet is not immune to physical theft. Therefore, you should ensure that you keep it safe. For instance, you can keep it in a safe deposit box. Since most paper wallet generators do not ask for personal information, most paper wallets cannot be traced to you. Below are some popular Ethereum paper wallets:

MyEtherWallet: Creating an Ethereum paper wallet using MyEtherWallet is quite an easy process. Simply head over to the MyEtherWallet website, create a password that will be used to encrypt your wallet and hit the download keystore file button. This will download an encrypted copy of your private key. From there, click on the print button to print your wallet. You will get a printed paper wallet that contains your wallet address and your private key. It will also have QR codes that you can scan to enter your keys whenever you want to transact.

ETHAddress: This is another popular option for creating Ethereum paper wallets. ETHAddress is an open source paper wallet generator that you can download on Github. The ETHAddress software generates a set of public and private keys which you can then print on a piece of paper. ETHAddress also gives you the option of generating an encrypted copy of your keys.

Mobile Wallets

These are wallets that allow you to access and spend your Ether from your mobile device. They provide the convenience of being able to access your Ether on the go. Mobile wallets are light clients, which means that, instead of connecting to the blockchain directly, they connect to other nodes in order to receive information about the blockchain. Mobile wallets are highly susceptible to hacking attacks and should only be used for storing small amounts of Ether. Below are some examples of mobile wallets:

Jaxx: This is a popular free Ethereum wallet that is available both on desktop and on mobile. Jaxx is compatible with both Android and iOS devices. Setting up your wallet with Jaxx does not require you to provide any personal information. Apart from Ether, Jaxx supports 15 other cryptocurrencies. One of the best things about Jaxx is that your keys are stored on your device and not on the internet. It also provides you with a seed key which can be used to restore your wallet in case you lose your device. The Jaxx interface is well designed and user friendly, even for absolute beginners. It also allows you to import your Ethereum paper wallet as well as to trade your Ether for other cryptocurrencies within the app.

Coinomi: This is another popular and well-reviewed mobile wallet that you can use to store your Ether, as well as several other cryptocurrencies. Coinomi is available for both Android and iOS devices. Like Jaxx, Coinomi stores your keys on your device. It provides you with a super-phrase that is used to back up your wallet. To keep users anonymous, Coinomi does not ask for personal information. It also has a feature that is used to make the IP addresses of its users anonymous. Finally, Coinomi is integrated with Changelly and Shapeshift, allowing you to convert your Ether into other cryptocurrencies from within the wallet.

Desktop Wallets

These are wallet applications that you install on your PC. Desktop wallets can either be full nodes that access the Ethereum blockchain directly or light clients that access the blockchain through other nodes. Light clients are easier to set up and less taxing on your computer's processing capacity. On the other hand, full nodes are much more secure, since they validate transactions directly from the blockchain. Setting up a desktop wallet is easy. They are also a lot more secure than mobile and web wallets. However, they are still susceptible to hacking attacks as long as your PC is connected to the internet. Below are some popular Ethereum desktop wallets:

Exodus: This is one of the best and most popular desktop wallets for storing your Ether, as well as several other cryptocurrencies. It has a well-designed interface that provides you with an overview of the amount of Ether you have in your wallet as well as their value in USD. While the Exodus wallet needs access to the internet, your keys are stored on your computer's hard drive. Exodus is also integrated with Shapeshift, allowing you to trade your Ether from within your wallet. For increased security, Exodus provides you with a seed key as well as one click email recovery, which helps you regain access to your Ether, in the event that you lose your private key. Exodus is free and is available on Windows, Mac and Linux.

Mist: This is the official Ethereum wallet. Mist is a full node wallet, which means that it will need to download the entire blockchain. Mist is available on Windows, Mac and Linux. Setting up your Mist wallet is a fairly easy process. After downloading and installing the application, you will be asked to create a password for your wallet. You should write down this password and keep it safe, since losing the password means losing access to your wallet. Using Mist is also quite straight-forward, although it is not as user friendly as Exodus. Like Exodus, Mist stores your keys on your computer's hard drive. Mist is also integrated with Shapeshift, making it possible for you to exchange your Ether for other cryptocurrencies from within the wallet. As the official Ethereum wallet, Mist also offers support for smart contracts.

MetaMask: Unlike the other desktop wallets discussed previously, MetaMask does not come as a standalone desktop application. Instead, it comes as a Chrome or Firefox extension. This means that is it available to all desktop users who have access to either Chrome or Firefox. Despite being a browser extension, MetaMask stores your keys on your computer's hard drive, which is why it qualifies to be categorized as a desktop wallet. One of the most outstanding features of MetaMask is that, in addition to allowing you to send and receive Ether, it also provides you with access to DApps running on the Ethereum blockchain. However, MetaMask does not support smart contracts. Shapeshift is also not integrated on the wallet.

Online Wallets

Also known as web or cloud wallets, these are wallets that are accessible over the internet from any device. As such, online wallets are the most convenient. However, they are also the least secure. This is because your keys are stored on the cloud, and in most cases, on third party servers. This makes online wallets vulnerable to all kinds of attacks. Additionally, since you are not in control of your keys, it essentially means that ultimate control over your Ether lies with the wallet provider. Accordingly, you should only use online wallets for storing small amounts of Ether. Below are some online wallets that you can use to store your Ether:

MyEtherWallet: Apart from being a paper wallet generator, MyEtherWallet also allows you to access and spend your Ether on the internet. However, MyEtherWallet does not work like other online wallets. Instead of storing your keys on online serves. Instead, it allows you to generate your own keys which you then store on your device. This makes it a lot safer than other online wallets. It also allows you to create and access smart contracts. MyEtherWallet also allows you to convert your Ether into Bitcoin. Since it is an online wallet, MyEtherWallet is accessible on any device that has internet access, including PS4. You can also access it on a computer using a hardware wallet.

Coinbase: Coinbase is a cryptocurrency exchange platform that also provides an online wallet. This is the most used cryptocurrency wallet in the world. Apart from Ether, Coinbase also allows you to store Bitcoin, Bitcoin Cash and Litecoin. However, the Coinbase wallet is not available in all geographical regions, so you should check on their website to confirm whether your country is supported.

Hardware Wallets

If you want maximum security for your Ether, your best bet is using a hardware wallet. Hardware wallets offer a mix of security and convenience. Hardware wallets look like conventional flash drives. However, they are specifically designed to hold your private keys. If you need to make a transaction, you only need to plug them into your computer and access your Ether. Since they generate and keep your private keys offline, hardware keys are not susceptible to hacking attacks. They are also password protected, which keeps your Ether protected even if the wallet gets stolen. Most also come with a form of back up that allows you to retrieve your Ether in case you lose your wallet. Below are some of the best hardware wallets for storing your Ether:

Ledger Nano S: This is one of the most popular Ethereum hardware wallets. The Ledger Nano S comes fitted with an OLED screen which allows you to set up and use the wallet without having to connect it to a PC. In addition to Ether, it also allows you to store Bitcoin, Litecoin and several other cryptocurrencies. The Ledger Nano S is password protected for complete safety of your Ether. It also comes with advanced security mechanisms which keep your Ether protected even if you use the wallet on a compromised PC. You can pick the Ledger Nano S from Amazon for about $100.

Trezor: This is another popular hardware wallet that was initially built for Bitcoin. However, it later added support for Ethereum. The Trezor uses 2-Factor authentication to for increased security. It also has in-built malware resistance features. It is accompanied by an intuitive interface that works n Mac, Windows and Linux.

Properties Of A Good Ethereum Wallet

With so many different types of Ethereum wallets to choose from, choosing the right one can be a bit confusing. The best Ethereum wallet for you depends on your needs and requirements. However, regardless of the type of wallet you decide to go for, you should check for the following factors:

Security: This is perhaps the most important thing when it comes to choosing an Ethereum wallet. Your Ether is equivalent to money, so you don't want to wake up one morning and find that someone has cleaned your wallet. Before using a particular wallet, perform your due diligence to ensure that it provides enough security. Some things to look at include the authentication process employed by the wallet, as well as where your keys are stored. If you opt for an online wallet, check whether the website has a secure protocol. Do this by checking whether the website has http or https. Avoid online wallets whose websites do not have https.

Multisig capabilities: Wallets that support multisig options allow you to use more than one private key to authorize transactions. This option makes a wallet more secure since a hacker will be unable to steal your Ether even if they manage to gain access to one of your private keys.

Anonymity: Sometimes, people want the ability to perform transactions without having to reveal their identities. If this is important to you, you should avoid wallets that user verification processes. There are several Ethereum wallets that allow you to set up your wallet without having to provide any personal information.

User experience: How easy is it to use the wallet? Is the interface intuitive? How easy or difficult is it to set up the wallet? Ideally, you should go for a wallet that is user-friendly and easy to use.

Reputation: It is always a good idea to see what other users are saying about a wallet before you start using it. This is where you find issues that will not be mentioned on the wallet provider's website. There are several cryptocurrency forums where you can check the kind of experiences other users have had with the wallet. You can also ask questions and get answers from people who have actually used the wallet.

Control over your Ether: This is another very important factor to consider. Remember, whoever has access to the private keys controls the Ether stored within the wallet. You should always go for wallets that allow you to store your own private key. Having access to your private key also gives you the ability to back up wallet without relying on the wallet provider.

Address Reuse: Some wallets require you to use the same address, while others generate a new address for every transaction. You should opt for wallets that create new addresses for every new transaction. Doing so helps to maintain user privacy.

Backups: Does the wallet allow you to make backups? If so, what kind of backup do they provide? How easy is the restoration process? Do they encrypt the backup? Do not use a wallet that does not provide a backup. In addition, you should use wallets that provide encrypted backups. Backups help you recover your Ether in case you lose access to your private keys or in case your device gets lost.

Cost: While most Ethereum wallets are free, some (such as hardware wallets) will need you to pay in order to use them. Is it within your budget to pay for a wallet?

Chapter Summary

In this chapter, you have learned:

- An Ethereum wallet is basically a piece of software that allows you to access your Ether, monitor your balance and conduct transactions.
- Your Ethereum wallet does not actually store any Ether. Instead, it stores your private keys, which gives you the ability to access and spend the Ether.
- There are several types of Ethereum wallets, such as paper wallets, mobile wallets, desktop wallets, online wallets and hardware wallets.
- A good Ethereum wallet should have good security, multisig capabilities, anonymity, good user experience, a good reputation, should provide a backup option, should use new addresses for each transaction, should be pocket friendly and should give total control over your Ether.

In the next chapter, you will learn some security best practices to keep your Ether safe.

Chapter Six: Security Best Practices To Keep Your Ether Safe

In this chapter, you are going to learn about some best practices you can follow to keep your Ether safe and secure.

Every few weeks, you will find reports on the internet about individuals and organizations who have been hacked and millions worth of cryptocurrency stolen. Cryptocurrencies have finally made money truly digital, opening it up to hacking attacks. A good example is the hack attack on The DAO, where more than $50 million worth of Ether was stolen. The rise of Ethereum to become the second largest cryptocurrency has attracted the attention of even more hackers, most of who were focused on Bitcoin. To make matters worse, Ethereum and cryptocurrency is still quite a complicated concept, even for people who participate in the industry, making it even more appealing to hackers. Therefore, it is important to make yourself conversant with security measures before you buy or start trading in Ethereum, or any other cryptocurrency for that matter.

However, before we get to the security best practices, I want to make a disclaimer. The Ethereum blockchain is as secure as can be, so there's no risk of hackers gaining access to the blockchain and making away with your Ether. For instance, when hackers hacked and stole from The DAO, they did not hack the Ethereum blockchain. Instead, they exploited a bug that they found in the code of The DAO itself. This means that the threat of hacking lies with the user as well as any third-party services they might be using to access their Ether.

Ethereum is a decentralized platform, which means that there is no one central entity that is in charge of ensuring that everything goes smoothly. This responsibility is devolved to all the users of the network, which means that the safety of your Ether ultimately lies with you. If you lose your private key, there is no central authority to help you regain access to your Ether. To minimize the risk of getting hacked and losing your Ether, below are some important things to keep in mind:

Store Your Own Ether

One of the things I have noticed is that when most newbies purchase Ether from a cryptocurrency exchange, they leave them in the wallet assigned to them by the exchange platform. This is a huge mistake. Remember, you do not have access to the private keys for that wallet, which means that you are not in control of your Ether. Every time you buy Ether from an exchange, always make sure to transfer them to a personal wallet whose private keys you control.

Perform Due Diligence Before Choosing A Wallet

While it is important to move your Ether to a wallet that you have control over, you should not simply move them to the first wallet that promises you control over your private keys. Take the time to perform your due diligence and find out whether the wallet is right for you. Does it provide the kind of security you need? Is it convenient for you? Can you afford it? Go through the factors discussed in Chapter Five and ascertain that you are picking the best wallet for your needs.

Use Cold Wallets For Huge Amounts of Ether

If you have a large amount of Ether, you should not store it in a hot wallet. Hot wallets, while convenient, are very vulnerable to attacks. Even if your wallet stores your keys in your hard drive instead of the cloud, hackers can infect your device with bugs that will crawl your hard drive looking for anything that looks like a wallet private key. If you want to store a large amount of Ether, find a cold storage, such as a hardware or paper wallet, since it is not vulnerable to hacking attacks.

Always Maintain Backups

The best way of ensuring that you do not lose a digital asset is to create a backup for it. This applies to all digital assets, from files and documents, to your Ether. This way, if you lose your device or your hardware wallet, you can still regain access to your Ether. For instance, most wallets provide a seed phrase that can be used to restore the wallet. You can copy this seed phrase on a piece of paper or save it as a text file in a flash drive. You should then keep the flash drive or paper backup safely. Do not store your backup in the same location with the main wallet. For instance, if you have Exodus on your desktop and then keep the backup in a flash drive in your bedroom, your PC and backup will both be destroyed if a fire guts your house. This beats the point of making the backup.

Ensure Your Wallet Is Password Protected

Most Ethereum wallets have the option of password protecting your wallet. Always make sure that you set up a password for your wallet. This keeps your wallet protected even in the event that a malicious person gins access to your device or your hardware wallet. When setting up a password, use complex passwords that cannot be guessed easily. Avoid using things like your favorite team, your nickname or your pet's name as wallet passwords.

Make Use OF 2 Factor Authentication

In addition to asking for a password to access your wallet, the best Ethereum wallets will also require an extra method of verifying your identity. This is known as 2 Factor Authentication (2FA). The extra method of authentication could be your fingerprint, a time-based one-time password or a confirmation code sent to your mobile device. 2FA provides an extra layer of security, making it impossible for malicious persons to access your Ether even if they steal your passwords.

Beware Of Scammers

Being a new industry and one that only few people understand, the crypto world is very vulnerable to scammers. This is also aggravated by the fact that the industry has turned some people into overnight billionaires. Scammers prey on greedy and clueless newbies trying to make an overnight fortune in the crypto industry. There are many kinds of cryptocurrency scams. For instance, in recent times, some scammers have been impersonating leaders such as Vitalik Buterin on social media and urging people to send a certain amount of Ether to a certain wallet in return for a larger amount of Ether. Others will ask you to 'invest' a certain amount of Ether, promising huge returns in a very short time. Do not fall for any of these scams or you will end up losing your Ether. Remember, when the deal looks too good to be true, it probably is.

Aside from scams that prey on people's greed, you should also watch out for phishing scams, which try to trick people into sharing their wallet passwords. These scams are especially rampant on email and Google Ads. Phishing scams try to present themselves as people you can trust with your login credentials. For instance, a scammer might email you trying to be your wallet provider, with a link to login to your wallet. Before clicking on any links, double check the source of the email to confirm whether the source is the actual wallet provider. Better yet, instead of clicking on the link, simply type the URL of the wallet provider into your browser and log in to your wallet from there. Similarly, do not click on ads when searching for your wallet provider on Google.

Chapter Summary

In this chapter, you have learned:

- The Ethereum blockchain is as secure as can be, so there's no risk of hackers gaining access to the blockchain and making away with your Ether. The risk lies with the user as well as any third-party services they might be using to access their Ether.
- Do not leave your Ether on the cryptocurrency exchange, since you do not control the keys to the wallet provided to you by the exchange.
- Perform due diligence before choosing a wallet.
- If you want to store a large amount of Ether, find a cold storage, such as a hardware or paper wallet.
- Always ensure that your wallet is backed up.
- Always make sure that you set up a password for your wallet.
- In addition to asking for a password to access your wallet, provide extra security by using 2 Factor Authentication.

- Always be on the lookout for scammers. Do not get into deals that seem too good or trust just anyone on the internet with your information.

In the next chapter, you will learn about Ethereum mining.

Chapter Seven: Ethereum Mining

In this chapter, you are going to learn what Ethereum mining is, how it works and what you need to become a miner. This chapter will also look at the profitability of Ethereum mining.

What Is Ethereum Mining

In the course of this book, I have mentioned the terms mining and miners, and you might be wondering what the terms mean. To understand what mining is, let us take a look at how transactions happen on the Ethereum blockchain. When you send some Ether to another user, your wallet broadcasts the details of the transaction to the Ethereum network. This transaction is grouped together with other pending transactions to form a block. Nodes within the network then try to confirm the validity of the block. To do this, these nodes must solve complex mathematical equations. The first computer to find a solution announces to the network that it has found a solution. While the other nodes in the network do not know the actual solution, they can confirm whether it is the correct solution by passing it through a hashing function. If more than 51% of the computers within the network confirm that the solution is correct, the block gets added to the blockchain. This system of achieving consensus is known as Proof of Work (PoW), since the node adds the block by proving to the others that it has worked to solve the complex mathematical equations. The node that found the solution is rewarded with newly released Ether, as well as the transaction fees for the block. This process of validating blocks and generating new Ether is what is known as mining.

The mining process is very computationally demanding. The nodes competing to find solutions to the complex mathematical solutions are essentially computers with high processing capabilities that are programmed to continuously run a hashing algorithm. The process of validating blocks within the Ethereum network takes about 12 seconds. After a block is added to the blockchain, the process starts all over again. By expending your processing power to mine on the Ethereum network, you can profit from the block reward (about 5 Ether) and the transaction fees awarded to you every time your computer mines a new block.

One of the key differences between Ethereum mining and Bitcoin mining is the hashing algorithms used by the two networks. Whereas Bitcoin uses the SHA256 algorithm, Ethereum uses an algorithm known as Ethash. Ethash makes it more effective to mine Ethereum using ordinary GPU's, unlike the SHA256 algorithm, which is more suited to ASIC's (Application Specific Integrated Circuits). ASIC's are very expensive, something that has made Bitcoin mining the preserve of the elite club of those who can afford ASIC's. Ethereum mining, on the other hand, is more decentralized, since GPU's are a lot more affordable.

Ethereum Mining Hardware

During the early days of the network, it was possible to mine Ethereum using an ordinary laptop or desktop PC. However, as more and more people started mining, the difficulty rate of mining Ethereum went on increasing to the point where it became impossible to mine using an ordinary PC. Today, if you want to get into Ethereum mining, you have to invest in the hardware to build a mining rig that has enough processing power.

To build a mining rig, the first thing you need to invest in is about six or more GPU's, the kind that are used for 3D video games. These GPU's should have a 3GB capacity or more. While it is still possible to use CPU's for mining, GPU's are more efficient since they are optimized for repeatedly running similar operations. Next, you need to find a motherboard for your mining rig. The motherboard should have at least 6 PCI slots for attaching the risers. You also need a power supply unit that will comfortably handle all the GPU's running simultaneously. The kind of power supply will be determined by the number of GPU's you decide to use on your rig.

The next piece of hardware you need to get is some powered risers. If possible, go for those that come with all capacitors built in. Risers will allow you to connect all your GPUs to the motherboard simultaneously. You also need to find a CPU and some RAM. However, since your mining rig won't be handling any multitasking tasks, the CPU and RAM need not be expensive. Finally, you will need a hard drive (about 60 GB or more will do), fans for cooling your rig and an Ethernet cable. You should not use your mining rig with Wi-fi.

Ethereum Mining Software

After you have assembled your mining rig, you will also need to install the software that will allow it to interact with the Ethereum blockchain. The first thing you need to do after building your rig is to install the drivers for your GPU. These can easily be downloaded from the manufacturer website. Some manufacturers will even provide the drivers alongside the GPU. From there, you need to install the mining software. There are several mining softwares that you can use for Ethereum mining, with the most popular being ClayMore Dual Miner.

You will also need to configure your rig as a node. This process will connect your rig to the Ethereum network and download the blockchain on your rig's hard drive. To configure use a tool known as Geth. If you want a simpler option, you can go with Ethermine or MinerGate. Once you finish configuring and connecting your rig to the Ethereum blockchain, you are ready to start mining. You can also perform other operations on the network, such as writing and executing smart contracts and building decentralized apps.

Pool, Solo Or Cloud Mining?

Now that your mining rig is ready, and your miming software has been set up, you are ready to become a miner. However, before you can get started, you need to decide how you will be mining. Ethereum mining usually takes one of the following three forms:

Pool Mining

This is the easiest and the most effective way to get started with Ethereum mining. Pool mining involves teaming up with other miners. Each of you provides their processing power to the mining operation. With the combined processing power, there is a higher chance for the pool to find block solutions than when you are working alone. This is a great way to ensure that you keep earning steady returns from your mining operations. Pool mining is also a lot easier for beginners, since there us a pool admin to help you solve any of the initial challenges you might encounter. However, you also need to keep in mind that mining as a pool means that you will have to share your rewards with the other members of the pool. The likelihood and frequency of finding block solutions will depend on the block size.

While I recommend pool mining, this does not mean that you should join the first pool you come across. Different pools have their advantages and disadvantages. Before joining a pool, there are a number of factors you need to consider. The first factor is the pool size. This is because the more the members within a pool, the higher the hashing power within the pool, which in turn means that the pool has a higher chance of finding block solutions. However, this also means that there will be more people to split the rewards with. All the same, it is a lot better to join a bigger pool. While your rewards per block will be certainly lower, you will be assured of getting regular rewards.

The second thing you need to consider is the minimum payout offered by the pool. The minimum payout refers to the smallest amount of Ether you need to accumulate before your payment is sent to your wallet. The larger the minimum payout, the longer you will have to wait before receiving your payments. I don't find this to be a good arrangement. Ideally, you should opt for pools that have a very little minimum payout. A small minimum payout means you will receive your payments more frequently. This gives you the flexibility of being able to quickly leave a mining pool if you feel that it is not the right one for you.

The next thing you need to think about is the pool fee. Being a member of a pool does not come for free. You have to pay a regular membership fee. These fees go to the pool administrator, since running a pool is basically a full-time job. The fees are also used for the expenses of running the mining pool. Pool fees are usually calculated as a percentage. The standard pool fee lies between 1% and 4%. Sometimes, you will come across some mining pools that have 0% fees. Such pools are usually supported by donations. However, they are not the most reliable, so you should opt for those with a fee of about 1% or 2%.

Finally, you need to consider the payment structure offered by the mining pool. The payment structures used by most mining pools can be divided into two major categories:

Proportional system: With this method, all the members receive a share of the block reward based on the percentage of hashing power they contribute to the pool. The more the hashing power you provide, the higher the rewards you receive.

Pay-per-share system: With this system, the payments do not depend on the number of blocks mined by the pool. Instead, the pool administrator calculates the number of blocks the pool is expected to mine in a certain period, based on the laws of probability. From this number, the administrator comes up with a fixed number of Ether that is paid to the members regularly. This means that, with the pay-per-share system, members receive steady returns whether the pool has mined blocks or not.

Solo Mining

If you do not want to mine as part of a mining pool, you can always go it solo. Mining solo means that you do not have to share your returns with anyone. However, you need to keep in mind that mining is a competition. All the miners are trying to be the first one to find the block solution so that they can win the block reward. You are in competition with all the miners, including those who have combined their hashing power together by forming mining pools. Therefore, as a solo miner, you have a very small chance of mining any blocks.

For you to succeed as a solo miner, you need access to hundreds of GPU's. Not only is gaining access to such resources wildly expensive, but you will also need to handle other problems. For instance, you have to build dedicated cooling systems for your multiple mining rigs to ensure that they don't break down from overheating. The noise from the rigs and dedicated cooling system also means that you cannot run such an operation from your apartment. This means having to get a warehouse or garage for your mining operation. In addition, your electricity costs would be extremely high. To avoid all these challenges while still running a profitable mining operation, it makes a lot more sense to join a mining pool.

Cloud Mining

If you want to mine Ethereum without having to handle the actual mining operation, you can opt for cloud mining. This is where you pay someone with the right equipment to do the actual mining for you. In other words, you are hiring their mining equipment and mining time. Initially, this might not look like a very logical arrangement. After all, why would someone who has invested in mining equipment mine for you instead of mining for themselves? However, cloud mining has a number of advantages to both parties. Since you pay for cloud mining services upfront, this is a way for the service provider to regain a guaranteed profit from their investment in mining equipment. On the other hand, paying for cloud mining services allows you to pass the cost of maintaining mining equipment to the service provider. For instance, if a mining rig breaks down, it is not up to you to purchase another one. You also do not have to build cooling systems in your home for your mining equipment or live with noisy equipment in your apartment. While cloud mining seems convenient, mining for yourself is more profitable, therefore I do not recommend cloud mining.

Can You Make Profits From Ethereum Mining?

So, is there money to be made in Ethereum mining? If you have the right equipment, you can make money from mining Ethereum. It's also good to keep in mind that the profitability of mining will also depend on some variable costs, such as the cost of electricity and equipment maintenance fees. Mining is an energy intensive operation. The lower you can keep your electricity costs, the more profit you will get from mining. The profitability of Ethereum mining also depends on the mining difficulty. The more people get into mining, the more difficult mining will become, which will lower miners' profitability. All in all, Ethereum mining is not a get rich quick scheme. However, you can make a modest amount of money per month from Ethereum mining.

It is also good to keep in mind that there are plans to shift the Ethereum network to a Proof of Stake (PoS) consensus system. This new system will not require nodes to solve the computationally demanding mathematical equations. Instead, they will be required to stake a percentage of the Ether they own in order to validate transactions. As the shift to the PoS consensus system approaches, Ethereum mining will become more difficult, which will in turn translate to less profits from mining. Once the shift is implemented, that will be the end of Ethereum mining, since the PoS system does not depend on mining to keep the Ethereum network running.

Chapter Summary

In this chapter, you have learned:

- Mining is the process of validating blocks on the Ethereum blockchain and generating new Ether.
- Nodes within the Ethereum network validate transactions by finding solutions to complex mathematical equations.
- The mining process is very computationally demanding.
- The major difference between Ethereum mining and Bitcoin mining is the hashing algorithms used

by the two networks. Bitcoin uses the SHA256 algorithm while Ethereum uses an algorithm known as Ethash.

- If you want to get into Ethereum mining, you have to invest in the hardware to build a mining rig that has enough processing power.
- After building your mining rig, you also need to install the software that will allow the mining rig to interact with the Ethereum blockchain.
- There are three major ways of mining: Pool mining, solo mining and cloud mining.
- Pool mining is the easiest and the most effective way to get started with Ethereum mining.
- You should always perform due diligence before joining an Ethereum mining pool.
- Solo mining is not a recommended option as it is costly and inefficient.
- Cloud mining allows you to mine Ethereum without having to purchase mining hardware. However, it is less profitable compared to mining using your own hardware.
- If you have the right equipment, you can make money from mining Ethereum.

In the next chapter, you will learn about investing in Ethereum.

Chapter Eight: Investing In Ethereum

In this chapter, you are going to learn everything you need to know about investing in Ethereum, including factors that affect the price of Ethereum, reasons why investing in Ethereum is a good idea, as well as the best method for investing in Ethereum.

Most people get into the world of cryptocurrencies because they want to invest and make themselves some money. If you are reading this book, chances are that you want to invest in Ethereum and make yourself some money. Since the invention of cryptocurrencies, people have seen very small investments turn them into millionaires and billionaires in the space of a few weeks. While this might seem unbelievable, it has become the norm in the world of cryptocurrency. Let's consider Ethereum for a minute. Since its launch, the price of Ethereum has grown by over 45,800%. In 2017 alone, the price of Ethereum skyrocketed from just above $8 on 1st January to over $760 by 31st

December. This represents a growth of almost 10,000% in a single year.

To put this into perspective, let's assume that someone has invested $1000 in Ethereum in January 2017. By the close of the year, their investment would have been worth $1,000,000. Our fictional investor would have become a millionaire within the space of one year, without doing much, just holding their investment. Such kind of returns is what has spurred even more people to get interested in investing in cryptocurrencies, and particularly Ethereum. In the space of a few years, Ethereum has established its space as one of the most fundamental platforms within the crypto ecosystem, and therefore, it is only logical to want a share of the pie. However, before we get into why investing in Ethereum is a good idea, let us first look at some of the factors that affect the price of Ethereum.

Factors Affecting The Price Of Ethereum

Before investing in Ethereum, or any other cryptocurrency for that matter, it is crucial to have a good understanding of the factors that determine the rise and fall of its price. It is also important to understand that there is a difference between the price and value of Ethereum. Value refers to the perceived usefulness of the Ethereum platform, whereas price refers to the exchange rate of Ether in relation to dollars, or any other currency for that matter.

Some of the factors that influence the price of Ethereum include:

Supply And Demand

Like any other commodity, the price of Ether is influenced by the universal market forces of supply and demand. These laws stipulate that when there is excessive supply of a commodity, the price will go down. On the other hand, if the demand for the commodity far exceeds the available supply, then the price will go up. So, how does this work in relation to Ethereum? The supply of Ethereum is capped at 18 million Ether per year. Regardless of whatever happens in the market, only 18 million Ether are released into the market each year. At the same time, the rate of demand for Ether is not constant. Different events either increase or decrease the demand for Ether. The main factor that affects demand for Ether is the media. For instance, if Ethereum receives positive news coverage in the media, more people become interested in buying Ether, which increases the demand, leading to an increase in price. On the other hand, if the news coverage is negative, it results in people wanting to get rid of the Ether they own. Since almost everyone is trying to sell, the price is forced to go down.

Trading

Most people buy Ether, not because they want to actually use the tokens on the Ethereum blockchain, but because they want to trade them on the cryptocurrency markets and make some money. You can compare cryptocurrency trading to stock trading. However, the cryptocurrency market is a lot smaller than the stock market, which means that the crypto market is more vulnerable to the influence of whales (large investors with huge sums of money). For instance, if a whale decides to offload a large amount of Ether, this can result in a panic in the market, leading to a fall in the price of Ether. Similarly, a large purchase of Ether by a whale in a short time will lead to an increase in its price. Sometimes, whales use such large buy and sell orders to influence the price of Ether by putting up what are known as buy or sell walls.

Government Policy

While most governments are yet to constitute any legal frameworks to regulate the use and trading of cryptocurrencies, some governments still pass some policies that have huge impacts on the price of cryptocurrencies. For instance, the banning of Initial Coin Offerings (ICO) by the People's Bank of China led to a fall in the price of cryptocurrencies, including Ethereum. Ethereum is the main cryptocurrency used for contributing to ICO's, therefore a ban on ICO's had a direct impact on the price of Ether. The price of Bitcoin also has a direct effect on the price of most other cryptocurrencies, so any government regulations that affect the price of Bitcoin are also likely to have an impact on the price of Ethereum.

Mining Difficulty And Profitability

The price of Ethereum is also dependent on the profitability of Ethereum mining operations. Mining profitability depends on a number of factors, including the cost of electricity, the current price of Ether, the price of mining equipment and the mining difficulty. As more people get into mining, the amount of hashing power expended into mining increases. To keep the rate of release of new Ether constant, the network reacts by increasing the mining difficulty. This means that to succeed in mining, miners must invest in higher end GPU's, which are more costly. This leads to a decrease in the profitability of mining. As a result, miners tend to hold on to their Ether for much longer in the hope that prices will increase in future. As more and more people hold instead of selling, this can lead to an increase in the price of Ether. Similarly, an increase in the costs electricity will lower the profitability for miners, causing them to hold their Ether.

Popularity Of ICO's

ICO's have gained prominence as a new and effective way for start-ups in the cryptocurrency sector to raise start-up capital. Most of ICO's are issued based on Ethereum's ERC20 token standard. This means that most of these ICO's take contributions in the form of Ether. For someone to contribute in an ICO, they need to purchase some Ether. As ICO's become more and more popular and as more and more people invest in ICO's, the demand for Ether also increases, resulting in an increase in price.

Why Investing In Ethereum Is A Good Idea

The factors discussed above are some of the reasons that the price of Ethereum rises and falls. With so many factors having a direct impact on its price, it is impossible to predict with accuracy the direction that the price of Ether will take. This means that investing still remains a risk. However, there are some factors that make investing in Ethereum a good proposition. These include:

Ethereum Has Wider Applications Than Bitcoin

One of the greatest selling points of most cryptocurrencies is blockchain technology, which makes cryptocurrencies secure, tamper proof and free from the control of banks and governments. By being the first project to propose a decentralized financial system that was outside the control of any nation, bank or government, Bitcoin gained a lot of popularity among cryptocurrency enthusiasts. Despite being so popular, the capabilities of Bitcoin are fairly limited. Bitcoin only provides a system that allows people to securely send and receive digital payments, and that is it.

Ethereum, on the other hand, is a lot more capable than Bitcoin. Ethereum expands on the technology introduced by Bitcoin to create a platform that has a level of flexibility and versatility that was unseen before. The Ethereum platform is a Turing-complete platform, which means that it can run any kind of code, given sufficient time and resources. This means that Ethereum can be used for all kinds of applications, in a wide range of industries and sectors, from finance and asset registration to democracy and voting. This means that, in the long run, Ethereum has more utility than Bitcoin. With applications spanning across industries, Ethereum is unlikely to fail. If applications in one industry do not work out, applications in another industry might gain widespread adoption. Therefore, by investing in Ethereum, you are investing in something that has demonstrated long term utility, therefore your investments are unlikely to go up in smoke.

Financial Institutions Have Adopted Ethereum

Like I mentioned in the previous point, Ethereum is suited for adoption across multiple and diverse sectors and industries. One of the industries that have shown great interest in the Ethereum platform is the financial sector. Whereas most cryptocurrencies are a threat to the banking sector, banks have realized that the Ethereum platform is something they can take advantage of to remain relevant despite the revolutionizing of the industry by cryptocurrencies. For instance, the Bank of America and Microsoft teamed up to create an Ethereum-based application that will improve the security of customer transactions. The application executes and encrypts customer transactions on the blockchain, meaning that only the involved parties can access information about the transaction, thus eliminating privacy concerns.

Despite Bitcoin having a big head start over Ethereum, the financial sector has always fought Bitcoin, instead of embracing it. However, they have seen the potential presented by Ethereum and have started forging collaborations with Ethereum. This adoption of Ethereum by big players within the financial sector will push its mass adoption. If you look at most new technologies, adoption is usually driven by huge industry players. Therefore, being embraced by the banking sector is like a guarantee for the eventual mass adoption of Ethereum. As more and more people and institutions embrace Ethereum, its value is definitely going to soar.

Stability

Another reason why it makes more sense to invest in Ethereum compared to most other cryptocurrencies is that the growth of Ethereum has been mostly organic. Compared to cryptocurrencies like Bitcoin, the price of Ethereum is relatively stable, devoid of sudden, massive spikes and falls. This means that investing in Ethereum is a lot less risky than investing in most other cryptocurrencies.

Great Team

Before investing in any cryptocurrency, it is essential to ensure that you invest in a cryptocurrency where you are sure that the team behind the project can achieve the vision and goals of the project. By investing in a cryptocurrency, you are basically betting on the objective of the project. For instance, when you invest in Ethereum, you are basically betting your money on the vision of Ethereum to become a global decentralized computer. If the vision is achieved, the value of Ethereum will soar, which translates to profits for you.

The team behind Ethereum is superb. At the helm of the Ethereum team is Vitalik Buterin, a young Russian-Canadian programmer. Buterin has been involved in the cryptocurrency space since 2011. In 2012, he participated at the International Olympiads and won the Bronze Medal in

Informatics. He was the cofounder of Bitcoin Magazine and has worked for both Egora, a cryptocurrency market and Dark Wallet. All these show that this is a guy who knows what he is doing. In addition to Vitalik, the team includes other people who have been involved in the cryptocurrency industry in various capacities. This is a solid team that is capable of delivering on the vision of the Ethereum project.

Fortune 500 Backing

In 2017, a group of major global companies came together to form the Enterprise Ethereum Alliance (EEA). The EEA is an organization whose goal is to identify the opportunities that the Ethereum platform presents for the corporate environment. At present, the organization has over 200 members, including companies like JP Morgan, Microsoft, Thomson Reuters, Intel and BP. The formation of the EEA can only mean one thing. These top companies have realized the huge promise that Ethereum holds. They do not want to miss out on this opportunities. During the early days of the internet, many of the companies in existence at the time were wary of this new thing known as the internet. They waited too long before coming aboard, something that cost them greatly. The companies that formed the EEA do not want to be left flatfooted as such a huge revolution happens. If such huge companies believe that Ethereum is going to cause a global revolution, then you can be certain it is something worth investing in. People are taking note of the EEA. Immediately after the formation of the Enterprise Ethereum Alliance, the price of Ether went up as crypto investors rushed to get into Ethereum.

Blockchain Improvements

Ever since its start, Ethereum had a well thought out timeline that would involve several upgrades along the way. So far, many of these upgrades have been implemented, improving the security and efficiency of the network. There are several other upgrades scheduled for implementation in the new future. For instance, there are plans to shift the Ethereum blockchain from a Proof of Work consensus system to Proof of Stake. Proof of Stake makes verifying transactions on the Ethereum blockchain more cost and energy efficient. Such upgrades make the Ethereum network more valuable, with a corresponding increase in the price of Ether.

Supported By Most Exchanges

When investing in cryptocurrency, it is a good idea to go for a cryptocurrency that has liquidity. This means that you should go for a cryptocurrency that you can easily buy and sell. Ethereum is highly liquid. The fact that Ethereum is supported by most cryptocurrency exchanges means that you won't have trouble finding a seller or buyer. Adding in the fact that it is supported by many exchanges pushes its adoption and makes it more widely acceptable.

What Is The Best Way To Invest In Ethereum?

Another challenge that most beginners face when they decide to invest in Ethereum is to determine the best way to invest. When it comes to cryptocurrencies, there are two ways of investing – HODLing and trading.

HODLing

HODLing is a term that is used to refer to investing in cryptocurrency for the long term. The term is an acronym that stands for Holding On for Dear Life. This basically means holding your investments for a long period (one year or more) without taking into account the short-term volatility of the markets. If your strategy is to HODL, all you need to do is to buy some Ether and keep them safe for a long period of time, waiting for the prices to grow. Once the price reaches your target, you then sell the Ether and take your profit. HODLing is generally considered to be the best strategy for beginners since it does not involve much. You don't have to spend a lot of time learning about the markets. Owing to the huge growth that can happen in the cryptocurrency world in the span of a year, you can make very huge profits by HODLing.

If you decide to HODL, the best time to enter the market is when the prices are significantly low. Observe the markets over several days or weeks and try to see if you can establish a trend. If the trend looks bullish, hop onto it and hold your Ether. To lock your profit, you can have a strategy where you sell portions of your investment every time certain price milestones are met. If you notice the markets turning bearish, take out your profits.

Advantages Of HODLing

Eliminate market noise: The cryptocurrency market is highly volatile. Prices keep swinging in the space of a few hours. Trying to time these short-term movements is no small task. However, if you analyze the market over a longer period, the market does not seem so volatile. You will notice gradual trends. When you hold your investments over the long term, you are basically ignoring these market noise and following a long-term trend.

Eliminate need for perfect timing: Like I mentioned in the previous point, the market is only volatile on a day to day basis, while it follows a general trend over the long-term. If you are trading on the short term, you must be perfect in your timing of the market. If you are a minute late, you might just get onto a bull run just before it tanks.

However, when you hold your investment for the long term, you do not have to be so perfect in your timing. Since trends take much longer to build up, you have enough time to hop onto the trend during a bull run.

Lower costs: When you hold your Ether for the long term, the only transaction costs you will pay will be the initial trading fee as you buy and the final trading fee as you sell. If you are trading on the short term, on the other hand, you are constantly buying and selling, sometimes even several times in a day. The costs from all these transactions can quickly ramp up into something significant. By holding, you avoid all these costs.

Less emotional strain: Trying to keep up with the high volatility of the cryptocurrency market on a day to day basis can lead to a lot of emotional strain, especially if you are not experienced. This is not to say that holding for the long term is not without its psychological strain. However, it is a lot less stressful than short-term trading.

Less taxing on your time: Holding your investment for the long term does not take a lot of your time. You don't have to keep monitoring the markets every single minute. You do not have to go through charts and technical analyses every single day. All you need to do is check your positions every few days and ensure that you stay on top of any major news affecting the crypto space.

Disadvantages Of HODLing

While holding your Ether for the long-term looks like a stress-free strategy, it has its disadvantages. These include:

- By HODLing, you cannot take advantage of the daily volatility in the price of Ether. Experienced traders might make more by short term trading for than you will by going long.
- Holding for the long term is basically betting that Ethereum will remain a dominant force in the cryptocurrency market. In the case that another cryptocurrency emerges and succeeds in edging out Ethereum, you might end up losing your investment.
- Some government policies might be passed that could cause a crash in the price of Ether. Therefore, it's a good idea to always keep abreast of any regulations affecting the crypto space.

Short Term Trading

If you do not want to wait for months or years before seeing any return on your investment, you can profit from taking advantage of the short-term volatility of the price of Ether. The idea is still the same as long term holding, only that it is implemented much more frequently. The aim is to buy when the price is low and wait for a short time rise.

Once the price increases significantly, you sell your Ether to lock your profits before the price falls again. Once it falls, you buy again and wait for another short-term rise.

Short term trading has its benefits. Owing to the high volatility, it is not uncommon to see 2-5% gains within a span of five to ten minutes. This presents a huge opportunity for significant short-term profit. If you are an experienced trader, you can make huge gains, even more than a long term HODLer. However, you should keep in mind that the huge opportunities are accompanied by equally huge risks.

The downside to short term trading is that it needs a lot of experience. You need a great understanding of the market and how it behaves. Without this understanding, you will probably end up losing your money. It is not uncommon to see inexperienced traders get into a trend just before it reverses.

Last Word On Investing In Ethereum

Investing in Ethereum, like other kinds of investments, is a very risky affair. If you are not experienced, you should proceed with lots of caution. Do not test the waters with both feet. Only invest amounts of money that you are comfortable losing. The best way to invest is to follow a hybrid version of HODLing, where you average in and out of trends in a reasonable amount of time (not too short, not too long). As you get more experienced at reading the market, you can then adapt your trading style to optimize your profits. If you decide to become a short-term trader, do not stake huge chunks of your portfolio in a single trade. Limit yourself to only a few trades each week.

Chapter Summary

In this chapter, you have learned:

- Cryptocurrency investing is an attractive option since it holds a promise of extremely big returns.
- The price of Ethereum is influenced by factors such as supply and demand, trading, government policy, mining difficulty and profitability and the popularity of ICO's.
- Ethereum is a great investment option since it has wider real-life applications than Bitcoin.
- Financial institutions have started adopting Ethereum, something that might spearhead the mass adoption of Ethereum.
- The price of Ethereum is a lot more stable compared to the price of most other cryptocurrencies.

- Ethereum is backed by a solid team that is capable of delivering on the vision of the Ethereum project.
- The formation of the EEA is a strong indicator that Ethereum holds a lot of promise for the future.
- Upgrades on the Ethereum blockchain make the platform more valuable, which in turn leads to an increase in the price of Ether.
- Ethereum is supported by most cryptocurrency exchanges, making it highly liquid.
- There are two ways of investing in Ethereum – HODLing and trading.
- HODLing is a great strategy for people who do not have a lot of experience in cryptocurrency trading.
- HODLing helps eliminate market noise, eliminates the need for perfect timing, has lower costs, has lower emotional strain and does not require a lot of time.
- By HODLing, you risk losing your investments in case a better cryptocurrency comes up or in case anti-cryptocurrency government policies are passed.
- Short term trading allows you to take advantage of the short-term volatility of the price of Ether. However, it needs a lot of experience.

Investing in Ethereum is a very risky affair. Always exercise caution and only invest amounts of money that you are comfortable losing.

Final Words

Thank you for taking the time to read this book, Ethereum: The Beginners Guide To Understanding Ethereum.

By now, you should have a very good understanding of what Ethereum is and the promise it holds for the future. Already the world's second largest cryptocurrency by market cap, Ethereum will make it possible for blockchain technology to be used in all kinds of industries and sectors, bringing a new revolution to the world of business, finance and computing. Ethereum promises to make blockchain technology mainstream.

Having completed this book, you are now equipped with knowledge that will help you take advantage of this newly emerging technology in order to make yourself some money. You have the knowledge you need to become a cryptocurrency investor. All you need to do now is to step out into the crypto world and start using this information to you advantage.

All the best as you start your journey into the world of Ethereum.

Finally, I would request you to leave an honest review for this book. Your feedback is greatly appreciated as it helps me to keep producing high quality services for you.

www.ingramcontent.com/pod-product-compliance
Lightning Source LLC
Chambersburg PA
CBHW052330220526
45472CB00001B/356